T0142748

Archway Publishing books may be ordered through booksellers or by contacting:

Archway Publishing
1663 Liberty Drive
Bloomington, IN 47403
www.archwaypublishing.com
1 (888) 242-5904

ISBN: 978-1-4808-6661-4 (hc)

Print information available on the last page.

Archway Publishing rev. date: 2/13/2019

Night Night Dance

A CLASSIC LULLABY

A Family's Wish

By James Stone

In The Beginning

Family's Surname

____

Mother's Given Name

____

Father's Given Name

____

Child's Given Name

____

Date of Birth

____

Place Of Birth

____

Length

____

Weight

____

Colors of Eyes

____

Color of Hair

____

Night Night Dance
A Classic Lullaby
A Family's Wish

1
James Stone
Night Night Dance
100 bpm
Piano
Night night dance Night night dance Time to do the
night night dance Go to sleep not a peep Time to do the
night night dance Night night dance Night night dance Time to do the
night night dance Momm -y's here Dadd -y's here With you as you sleep
Night night dance Night night dance Time to do the Night night dance
Soft kisses and pleas -ant dreams will be here when you a -wake We will be
here with you al - ways

Night Night Dance

Night Night Dance

Time to do The Night Night Dance

Go to Sleep not a Peep

Time to do The Night Night Dance

Night Night Dance

Night Night Dance

Time to do The Night Night Dance

Mommy's Here

Daddy's Here

With you as you Sleep

Night Night Dance

Night Night Dance

Time to do The Night Night Dance

Soft Kisses and Pleasant Dreams

We Will be Here with You Always

Weekly Experiences

1st

2nd
3rd

4th

5th

6th
7th

8th
9th

10th

11th

12th
13th

14th

15th

16th

17th

18th
19th

20th

21st

22nd

23rd

24th

25th

26th

27th

28th

29th

30th

31st

32nd

33rd

34th

35th

36th

37th

38th
39th

40th

41st

42nd
43rd

44th
45th

46th

47th

48th

49th

50th

51st

52nd Birthday

Night Night Dance
A Classic Lullaby
A Family's Wish